D1527086

Laws of My Nature

Also by Margot Schilpp

The World's Last Night

Laws of My Nature

Poems by
Margot Schilpp

Carnegie Mellon University Press
Pittsburgh 2005

Acknowledgments

Many thanks to the editors of the following publications where poems first appeared.

Black Warrior Review: "Equilibrium"; *Blackbird*: "Spring Burials"; *Connecticut Review*: "Ghost Ships" and "Courting the Horizon"; *Chelsea*: "In the Parlor of Instructions: Want" and "Taking Leave of My Senses"; *The Cincinnati Review*: "Journey"; *The Cortland Review*: "After the Cocktail Hours" and "For the Cormorants Whose Necks Are Loosely Tied with String So They May Not Swallow Their Catch"; *Fine Madness*: "Never-Never" and "American Blue"; *The Journal*: "What Narrative Is For"; *Natural Bridge*: "What I'll Know"; *NIMROD*: "Reaching Danger"; *Pleiades*: "Laws of My Nature"; *POOL*: "Ouija"; *Shade*: "Of Stars and Water and Instructions for Observing Both" and "Knowing"; *Tailwind*: "Poem in Which I Am My Evil Twin," "My Compass Will Not Orient," and "True North"; *Third Coast*: "Vantage Points," "Trompe l'Oeil," and "In Which the You Is Multiple"; *Valparaiso Poetry Review*: "If You Agree I'm Telling the Story," "Revisiting Gauguin," and "Words a Hospitality."

"Laws of My Nature" was featured on *Verse Daily* (http://www.versedaily.org) on July 4, 2002.

My gratitude to Yaddo, where many of these poems were conceived or completed.

The publication of this book is supported by a grant from the Pennsylvania Council on the Arts.

Library of Congress Control Number: 2003112554
ISBN 0–88748–420–4
Printed and bound in the United States of America
Book design and composition by Richard Foerster

10 9 8 7 6 5 4 3 2 1

Contents

What Narrative Is For

How fine the mind that can calculate
change and recognize destiny,

as if luck had something to do
with knowing, as if the lease

signed with the eyes closed
meant happiness, or even time

that's bearable, slow breaths exchanging
the currency that wanting spends,

and how fine that sedatives
and jewels exist, those slanted elegies.

So there are errands and hours
when you hear your own breath—

or feel my breath coming from within you—
and register the haunt of cicadas

summering under the porch. So there is time
spooking off into the wings.

These are going to be big surgeries, bloody
gauzes of conditions, when loss

must be measured, and then
there are the outcomes, the calls

that must be made. Wouldn't we all like to avoid
being the reason for anguish, to understand

why it's so easy to cut ourselves
on our own edges? Silent,

the responders. They might
have the answers, but they're not

telling, even when the vise grips
go for the nails. All that's left is to know

we will suffer through almost anything—
make sure to remember it well.

Taking Leave of My Senses

I want that, I think, when I see the slender body
of the model, the deer's white tail,

the hood ornament that glints
in the strong sun, day after day,

all the traffic of memory knotted
up in a big jam, resistant to weaving in

or out, standstill of the synapse,
standstill of the heart, the skipped beat

in a chamber of its own. Some things
just are: the seagull, the pocketbook,

the wrought iron gate around
the fierce heart. I want that, I think,

when I see you running up the path,
your world proportioned through earphones.

You're listening to Bach, or some torchy song
that brought a generation of women

to their silk-stockinged knees. *You can't
always get what you want*, even if

it would bring a few hours of rapture.
I can't see the harm in imagining

tracing my tongue slowly up
the side of your neck or

for one small moment introducing
my hands to every inch of your back.

I can't see the danger in merely thinking
myself spread open and meeting you

on the downswings. The story is old:
two by two, Noah and his wife, all the animals

paired off and going gently
up the planks—the story is unlikely.

The doe was thinking of the ten-pointer
she'd passed in the woods.

The ewe was fixating on all the wool
she'd had to leave behind. The lion shook

his great mane into the wind, sniffed
the air for other possibilities.

This is my brief sedition. This is my
resistance to the order of things,

to what I thought of as the one
way my life could be lived, my body's

autonomic reaction against what I've agreed
to, for ever and always, my little

mutiny against the status quo
of hearing—at the toy store, in

the checkout lines, in galleries
and churches—the harsh whispers

of all our mothers saying,
You can look, just don't touch anything.

Journey

The dragonflies braid themselves in and out
of the air—a riot of wings and destinations.

This could have been a figure of speech;
it could have been a lie.

But it might have been everything,
in that instant, and then what if it were over—dirty

water circling the drain—about to go down,
about to disappear into the grammar

of pipes that draws things away from us?
So I waited until the dawn came.

I gave up eating and sleeping and washing
my hair. I didn't feed the dog.

Who would come along with an oar?
Who might happen by with a switchblade

and a bottle of icy beer?
And this might be the only time I'll ever feel like this.

It might be the future, when everything
still happens, but it's always more intense.

That world allows us.
That world is a weird parallelogram,

a slanted view—things I recognize exist
there, yet they are changed.

I know my life
is about to become the funhouse mirror—

incredible distortion, bare recognition.
Is that me? Is that? Of course. I'm watching

myself evolve—I'm a piece of rotting fruit,
a chameleon resting on a new log.

It wants to happen gradually.
It wants to happen now.

So I'm taking all of this down
to remember when I lose my courage:

see the way the rain comes down—
inevitable and destined to be

wherever it arrives. That's me—
the drop contained for now.

Destiny sits beside me
on the couch and taps my shoulder.

I try to ignore him, but he's persistent
and he knows what's going to happen.

I'm on my way out the door.
I'm on my way, and out the door.

Come with me into my life:
I've brought kettledrums and paste,

lacewings and a canteen of water.
I've brought a box full of odd buttons.

I'm carrying a stick I've carved into
the shape of a stick.

I have my memory of the image
of the dragonflies navigating.

And for when you're angry,
I've brought my tongue and the details

of some argument we've yet to have.
For when you're hungry, I've brought

my lips and the soft skin
along the back of my neck.

If You Agree I'm Telling the Story

The capiz shells chime in the wind, and would
destroy me if I weren't armed: I have denial
and an armada of recollections that prove

there were balloons
and paper plates with pieces of cake.
I hear the sounds of children's shoes.

I see the lit candles, hear the singing that's begun.
It's an ordinary day, nothing
to alarm, nothing to frighten or warn.

They walked through the market and she chose
wind chimes for her souvenir. All the way home
her bag would not be quiet.

Think of any sentence
and attach to it a meaning:
Brad walks to the store. [Brad is leaving.]

Mary has lost her keys. [Mary has some
deep psychological problem that prevents her
from remembering where she puts things.]

The sky is blue. [The sky looks blue to us,
or what we all agree to call blue.]
We lack imagination more than we lack

consensus. So, yes, call the sky blue.
Call things by the names they've been
assigned—memory, birthday, patent leather,

wind chime—and the story can continue.
Under the high windows, a garden hose
coils. Across the street, a dog barks. I told you

it was an ordinary day. You trust me,
don't you? Trust me to tell you
what you need to know? I will.

I will: a huge crystal vase,
the tiny wrist of a child.
Talk of stitches.

Talk of scars. The party's over
and I've told you nothing.
I forgot to mention all the blood.

Of Darwin, the Color Green, and Spring's Arrival

We go outside to check the traps.
March and the false arrivals
of weather seduce us
into thinking winter's over.
One more little drama

in the huge production, one more
false witness against you at your trial.
It's a plague, this alternation
between polar bears and tadpoles,
penguins and hatchlings, and

I never remember last year, so
each year this happens anew.
There's winter disappearing
like a freight train around a bend,
there's spring arriving, looking

for a taxi into town. The water's
clear edges announce
the margins of the lake, though
I'm no Narcissus, look down not
to find my own reflection, but

to see the water scatter inside itself.
More rain and green everywhere,
which reminds me of algae, of Darwin
and how he must have longed
for something beyond

the *Beagle*'s confines; green
waters lapping at the margins
of the ship, green stomachs turning
themselves inside out over
the decks, green

foliage proving the theory
and the fact of every garden
everywhere, this return,
this hypothesis: we survive
each year to forget the last and in

our amnesia can discover it
all again, even the ferocity
that passes for kindness in this
world gone and
gone mad.

Trompe l'Oeil

Tomorrow and tomorrow, gentlemen,
yet there's only today to notice
how in a city without money,
kisses can buy you
a song or an hour of having

honeydew melon rubbed into
your skin. It shouldn't take so long
to realize the city is
on fire: vision happens badly, your eyes
tricked into not remembering

depth. Patterns soak into you,
and that's all you have.
Simple, to define what is wrong
and know it is so. Harder
to refrain. See the illusion

overtake you, wash over
you like the end of youth, over
the setting sun dangling like a kite
in the trees, then lower,
a refinement of a web, a scar,

a distance that orders soldiers
to the fields. They do not want
to go. Their families love them.
Their blood resides inside their skin.
Then, into place, the hours.

And how berries taste when
you're in love. The world owes
you the admiration of children
and dogs, the story behind the story.
Stay to discover lycanthropy

and silence and the voodoo
of satin peeling away
from skin. I can't go around thinking
there is more—there's just now,
these words, these veins on this leaf,

that are here, then will vanish into
the amnesia of the hours. But doesn't
it all look real? Doesn't it fool the eye
into constructing a finer work?
A trick of pigments: one stroke

here, another, then a whole building
or city or scene projects into the universe.
Far, the shore of home, slow the hours to get there.
The oriole transports an earthworm,
the bowerbird, sticks to lure

his love—most animals take home only
what they can carry in their mouths—
but we must bear the weight of many hearts
to protect us from the winds
that gather, from the idea of heaven.

American Blue

You can't say I have no imagination
when all I can think is blue,

blue, blue: the car's wheels touching
on blue asphalt, the trellis of cerulean roses,

the schizophrenic aqua of the flame
devouring the heretic's heels,

but isn't there more to this palette
than loneliness? Doesn't the wide

Missouri flow up the Continent
into our minds' lakes? I hope

one day there's medicine for treating
America, but for now, it's all

boot soles and gravy, flags and fields.
The tongue finds the easy answer: *Yes,*

and don't you forget it. I wasn't always this
close to breaking apart, wasn't

always one step from the
circular saw, the wagon wheel,

the fruit bowl crashing across
the mantel. There used to be order.

There used to be significance
in the arrangement of objects,

the invitations to guests. Now
all the china has petal–shaped chips,

and here are all the warped candles,
shattered legs, broken songs fetched down.

If we all shrug down to our knees,
maybe we won't completely burn

during the hottest part of the day.
Say no to the formula: one and

me makes me and another
something or someone, minus me,

leaving them so blue.
Now, the incandescence of true

lights the way—I am spoken. I am
the spoke, the bread, the flagstone

by which early morning's chill
cools the bluest air.

What Isn't Real Is Real Enough

*. . . And then the fountains poured water out into
the pools. And the water was black, was green, was
shocking blue that described blue and became blue. I
saw this with my own eyes: I was the recollection,
was the myth, was the woman brushing her long,
long hair down from the stones of the tower . . .*

Worn out, thinned down, true
of ax and blade that spin
out of the sky, this natural
dark spent on years of coaxing

the dog to run its path,
the raven to fly higher,
and in moments when
doxology fails, when the chants

no longer lure you to your knees,
it's time to prohibit looking back—
they'll take your money,
give you back a glass slipper,

a pea, a wound in your palm,
or a kiss that stuns you.
Yet the organs fail in the failing
light, the obsolete gesture,

the wave goodbye, and all
along you were always leaving.
So it hasn't seemed like mystery
in any sense or at any time—

you thought you knew outcomes
and promises you made, even
if one hand was tied behind
your back with pink satin

and your beautiful eyes were closed.
Even if someone blew up
a garbage can in the next scene.
Even if loitering were forbidden.

You believed the stories
of the golden goose, the sullen
nature of the wolf. You believed
in migration, in the happy ending.

Now the rules of engagement confuse
you: hear the insistence on taking
no stance but the paths to preservation,
to saving what's left of what little

there was in all of this—tornadoes
of guilt and gusts of atonement.
The door blows down—it is hinges
and hardware and plank. How fierce

the winds that can move a heart.
How fine the monuments
that memory erects in the place
of what really happened.

The other side is visible from where
I'm standing, even if heaven is opaque.
Even refuge must stand still
sometimes to assess the degrees of misery.

River of Me

Everyone I love is far away,
beyond image
or conversation, beyond
hearing, but not past
memory, that flower
that blooms inside
and needs almost
nothing to make it last—
over time, over distance,
over over, and still, the mislaid.
Simple to complete
the circuit, and doesn't the earth
want our attention,
want to show us
how we can be the future
of ourselves, a dark road
lit by the candles of yes?
If once the trees
were animate, like tides,
I'd fold up my heart's tent
and go farther into
the desert: see our names
hanging across the branches
of the trees, and know
the birds pronounce *Margot*
and again *Margot*, and then
I'm swimming across
the landscape,
mindful that distance
can clarify as easily
as it destroys, its power
rising up the banks,
out of control, but true.

In the Parlor of Instructions: Want

If things do not make sense, upend them.
Here is a carton of mild, here is a swan
swimming in honey.
Perform a circular pantomime of the self,
a bearing of your other self—to point
in the direction of the wind,
of the window, of the winding sheet,
of the shroud, of the sheet, of the music,
of a small child's
small hand, of another hand
that bludgeons or caresses,
or smooths the wrinkles from a piece of paper
onto the secret darknesses
when there's no one looking.
I wouldn't want this kingdom
with its crown and scepter that never cool,
with its queen reigning over grief.
This life, a mending. A bleed.
A bomb. And in the predicament of altruism,
you give. In the circumstances of temptation,
you may not yield. The orphan
of desire wings toward
you: and you want and want. You wanted.
Consider want as the noun, but also as the verb,
as the original
beauty of having a direction.
Cast off into the tradewinds of distance.
Raise up your flag in surrender
to the violence, the escapes
from the visual field. Find
there's nothing but some politeness
inhabiting the space of reason. Bow
low and open your eye and other eye, not

a wink, but a sequence. Not a word,
but a song, a silence, a wingspan of otherness
folded over the best parts of this life,
the sadnesses in the veins.
Want in the openness
of things, in the shadows and blindnesses,
in the blessings (of course),
to be said, into the handkerchief of our days,
to disguise our voices (of course), though
we have yet to hear them.

Courting the Horizon

It's a night to recall storms:
the way the gullies are rocked

with ice and wind, the hail
that dents cars and the matchsticks

striking at all odd hours,
when dusk hasn't fallen yet,

when the flame hardly matters,
though in the darkness—in absolute darkness—

it would, and would be a damn good thing,
too. Three-on-a-match was a no-no, too much

time for the enemy to sight and shoot,
though we can stand around on our corners

all day and take time to light things up—
even the canoes of memory that slur

out of the dimness require more
than matchlight to illuminate

the furthest corners of what happened
a year or two ago, or yesterday.

I wanted a little glamour,
and the morning toast's not the place

to find it, not unless the toast is encrusted
with diamonds and cut into the shape

of a crown, a Lamborghini, or the heart
of the woman who loves you. Maybe stillness

causes these digressions while it exhibits
the patience of an old woman,

a pregnant cat, a lawyer
waiting for his money.

It's close to legend how the early signs
of falling out of something are a loss

of balance and a quick change of scene—
blink and you're somewhere else—

the circus, a strip joint, on the ground
in the alley behind Henri's Bistro.

Blink and the horizon reconfigures,
which is something like what can happen

if you're not careful with your checkbook
or car maintenance or to whom you tell

the secrets of your past. That horizon
reconfigures into a new vista

in which you must have faith—the old
one's gone and won't be returning,

the tides of regret or contentment
washing up ever so slightly lower

each time you check, until they reach
their ebb. What if the only thing

keeping you from falling on purpose
is the current horizon, the one you know

and have come to rely on,
the one you can't let go of, yet?

Of Stars and Water and Instructions for Observing Both

Sometimes it's best to understand nothing,
unless you can see how, in the future, it's all going
to come crashing into the water—the gory end
of things, the blood and the tall, cool glasses
lined up around the pool's lip, where the body floats,

bobs, really, with the uncontrolled movement
of lack. Lack of breath. Lack of volition. If floating
like that is the only tragedy you ever encounter,
it's enough. You shouldn't have to fear anything
else, but doesn't living interfere with that ambition?

Every day new calamities to consider, every
day new messes made in the haphazard
way of thoughtless grace—you make me,
for instance, see that my entire orbit
has been around the wrong planet,

that my calculations were off from the beginning.
I'm no astronomer, the stars guide me
by existence, not position,
since charts and visions by their natures
are contradictory. I'm a master at contradiction:

witness the lonely and satisfied heart I carry
behind my breast, the topsy-turvy signals
battling it out in my skull—none of this
would have happened if not for appetite—
how long since I stood inside myself and felt

my skin fit? All the hungers rising up—
like a telescope pointed at the right star, the one
where an event will occur that shakes up
the community of science, the stargazers,
the kids necking in a car, even the raccoon

crossing the road and disappearing
into the denseness of the forest—all the hungers
for knowledge or passion or change, or simpler
things, a glass of orange juice
and a piece of buttered toast—all of this

reminds me of dislocation. All of this reminds me
how many blank pages are in the book.
There's a different remedy for every ill,
but you can also use the same one every time:
know yourself. Which symptoms will respond

to touch. Which you can ignore and hope
will go away. But there's still the corpse
in the pool, the floating specter of your life
that has to be fished out. Face what's next:
Grab the net. Make all the necessary calls.

What I'll Know

What I'll know years from now is that certain facts
mustn't desert me: the memory of my body

when it was young, the way my heart
squeezes at the arrival of the moon, how

snow falls in a loud, wet hush. Nothing
on earth directs me more than sense,

the deep signals blinking stop or go. I have
to pay attention to the lilac melody or crown

of sonnets that plays across the keyboard
of my ear. So many disasters, so many fugues,

our collisions—these should be obvious and
in the perfect world, decisions would be easy:

pink or blue, paper or plastic, the life I have
or the one I construct out of feathers

and the rocks hanging against the sky.
In the far corner of desire, your hands

presume to know better, but once the shades
are pulled down, there's another lesson

in that privacy: you must do
everything you dream of, and more,

must be willing to go beyond the surface,
beyond treading water until the currents

change. Watch me when I kiss you: you'll
know something enters your heart, and

couplets, I might remind you, are a natural
choice for the love poem, for figuring

out what two means, especially when
chameleon and echo stand for the impulse

to believe, for the wonder of how we make
ourselves think original and blend and adapt.

What chord could I play that only you
would hear? What molecule the one

I would know you carried in a branch
of your left lung forever? I'm only

trying to convince myself I can endure
without everything I suddenly realize

I want: your arms around me, the rest
of my hours slipping under this avalanche

of words, and all the scales tipping
in the opposite direction, where everything

reminds me of birds, of their beautiful
flutterings in the heart's lonely season.

Takeover

Heartsound: thunk and paddle
up the stream of appetite that cloaks

me in sleep. In the split
of my personality, there's you and

everything else, all the parallelograms
and missiles hiding in the silos.

Or deep, way down in the water,
you'll find the torpedoes, their mischief

and fickle heads, thinking
about the kill, the kill. If

our nights together aren't to be, why
play awake during the day?

Duck your head if you're too tall
to enter the familiar

nothing of regret. You'll fit.
You'll fit nicely. I'm going

back to origami and the alphabet,
where order reigns. I'm going

back to original sin, where at least
I'll have a sense of humor.

This life splits me:
one half, red. The other,

blue. Very red. Very blue.
But I can conjure. I can cast. I can bring

you in. The weeds in my garden
have it all over the perennials.

Ouija

The letters spell water
so I think to avoid it. I shun
baths, travel over land.

Nothing's by logic
here. Intuition rules, not
a butterfly, not a zombie

or a house without doors,
the merciful blank
or its outcome.

The letters spell food,
so I eat. Later, act.
So I audition, absolutely

me. Suppose has
something to do
with consequence

and need, which are fabrics,
sheets drawn tight around me.
Worshipful at the estuary,

strange seemed
a strange sight.
The letters spell longing.

Know of the pine.
Know of the berry.
I make a pile of leaves

in the dark, spread them
down the hallway.
I bring them in,

but say no,
wanted to be
wanted another hour

and a candy of flesh
to roll in my mouth.
Wanted eyes I could put

in my back pockets.
Wanted collapse
and decadent to conflate

within me, to limitless,
to time, to water, to dark
longing in your hair.

Wanted chewing on me.
Stars all across.
The letters spell salvage.

Desired a robot for the moment.
And a tree, and a white fox dashing
across the dreams.

Wanted flight and
passage. Skin I could not lose.
Wanted more of being

a curvature of thought, a true,
a knot. Wanted
to be caught up, wanted dusk,

wanted sheets to sweat into.
To mummify. To thaw. To be
wanted exactly so.

Laws of My Nature

Obviously, the roosters are in league
with morning, the thrum of the sun
placing itself into the sky, again

the cholera, and again, mitosis—
electric salts of friction and desire
that appear out of nothing. Obviously

this happened, though as in dreams,
there are moments that feel
it might not have, not a dream, not a dream,

not anything, really, except disappearing
into silence. Regret is not a drug
I take, and so I'm still sane. I am indigent,

which means to be in want, yet I want
for nothing. Another citadel of the skin,
another who can name me. Close by,

this waterfall carries breath.
I am enamored. A reverie continues.
Blue is an endearment, erratic

and sometimes missing. Let me decide
to speak, and then I am saying love,
I am saying again and everything and

absence, into the heavy air, almost
a fabrication of air, until it moves
into the lungs darkly. There is solace

in understatement, even if a thought
continues unsaid. There is the opposite
of clamor, and surely there is always

one feather spiraling on the wind.
I worry when things seem true,
and so disbelieve. I surrender

to the hardness of slate
and to the mossy places. Do you recognize
the markers of yearning in disguise?

Can you understand momentum
while you stand perfectly still?
A snake drops from the tree and makes

a small noise—the sound of thinking
itself away—and across the leaves,
a slithering. My conscience must operate

that way—a long drop and then evasion—
because to understand how longing works
I would deny the sun its rising.

Poem in Which I Am My Evil Twin

You'll think I'm imagining things:
the copper taste in my mouth, the ghosts

of your hands. So, the world completes
another turn, another day of wishing

the frames could be removed from in front
of the pictures. Take away the one

for secrets, take away the one for lies.
Take away the one marked "only you,"

the one for "holier than thou." Start
to see something—a song rising into a fist.

There's not a trace left of last night
or the nights before, the awl pulled

from the back or the family money.
Everything vanishes, everything goes still.

You'll think the days and nights
can be the same. I'm here to tell you

it's true: things are no different
but not the same, since my cells beat

a path to your door. I'm here to tell you
it's fine. The order is in place:

there's still the one about the cigar,
the check is still in the mail.

Words from East of West

Oh to be the well   the portent
of a future
        passing between
    us, and
of sunset:
            change,
    chance,   rock or simple
memory that forestalls   divinity
in the open door
in the open palm
the heart's lavishings,
reading the leaves   for the apple
for the icepick, pomegranate, witch-stick,
        dunce.
                Said never.   Said yes.
Came upon you slowly.
Found lava and ash.
Didn't know better.
Hadn't.   Said please.
Said thank you.
                    Again.
Start over.
Reclined in spirit.   Drove to town,
    milk, eggs, paper
        the things
brought down.   Easy to recognize
                sadness: weeping.

East of grief, the writing on the walls,
                                messages sent
down
    of prosperity and kindness.

The erasures.   The lacunae.
                What missing is.

If the tide continued to rise over us.
                If the sun stuck in the highest part
                                    of the sky.   Apogee.
Apologies.
                The wound hidden in a sleeve,
under shirt button or tie.
     But it bleeds.   Stitches apart.
I sent a message to the gods:
                                I have not finished here.
No reply yet,
        but even
over the brightness
                of the moon
and music falling from across the lake's creation—
that story wound through me.
                                In every place
the minutes unwind.

Exile

Arc of a petal falling,
arc of a playing card,
                arc of whale's fin or
monarch wing,
                curve of beach
        where tropical crabs
                come alive in the sand's sultry heat.
Waves and palm fronds sing,
strategize: it's paradise
        when the frame obstructs
the remnants of an experiment gone all to hell:
                hollows of memory
                        absorb secrets and lie,
fallow, in the mists of a garden where you could once give
or bravely take the news:
I'm bankrupt, but can tell the story.
Once . . .
                . . . revelation . . .
                . . . and then . . .
                . . . revelation . . .
. . . denouement.
        I'm sitting in the third row, breathing
lightly, saving air.
This morning, the painted
                lanes change into rivers, nails,
                                cats poised
in attack stance. Whatever's walking down
the sidewalk toward you
whispers past, but I am possessed
by knowledge:
        death a coin we spend
                                just once
and no currency to buy fidelity,
                                even blessed

all night, when so much music passes,
there may be another
you choose
            to adore.
Leave it to the experts—don't try
        this at home.
I have felt every bone, which ones
                        are weakened by beauty.
No detail not worth applause
in the dark, and lately
                    mangoes in my dreams.
Lately, spicy food,
ribbons braided in my hair,
accoutrements weighing me down
                    so I don't float
            away.
                Some mornings,
I'm thinking fireworks, a Lear jet
to Paris for lunch with Karl or Paloma, a brief
walk up the Left Bank to look at art, really look
        at what other people's eyes
are telling their minds they see:
                the impulse guided down the arm
and out the hand, in smudges
        of gray or blue or pink,
nearsighted love of drama
                and cathedral, fog lifting,
the river's sleepy turns
and meanderings
        past stone bridges, brown
                wrought iron that outlines balconies
and windows, all
of this wanting
to be color or light,
from the scallop
        along the hands
                and from the contours
of the mouth,

that asks which of the shapes,
which of the colors,
    which of the details,
will you choose
to represent
            what's chosen you?
Paint me into the corner—
abandoned warehouse,
    goldenrod field,
            thistle-covered hills—I don't care
if I'm only a shadow,
    as long as I know I'm there.

Solving for the Plain Truth

Where the dirt road ends,
canisters of tear gas are propped

up on an old couch, which the lace
shadows of the trees cover like doilies,

so there is beauty here, and this must be
where it was concealed all along, even

while you were looking for it
in the contour of a thigh, in the slopes

of many breasts. What better view
than this one, and who more right

to it than you? The art of observation lies
along the unmarked road to faith

and you are a believer. But I am weary
of running away from the wilderness

to find true images that matter.
I call the mango and nutmeg divine,

chop the skins of many onions. I only cry
into the night's persuasive air

because whole continents are turning
their faces to the sun, or because

the instructions to solve for x
left me with a headache and a hunger

for what's simple, which is to say nearly
everything, really, when you break

it all down into details or components
or stages, though the wind defies this,

with its genesis nowhere and its abrupt
not anymore. To understand simplicity,

shouldn't I know how wind begins?
Shouldn't there be some answer in the trees?

Vantage Points

I don't believe in fables
unless the hero dies.
What happiness I find,

I find inside
the terrors of the heart,
the body chosen

for the night.
I like it that there's not a bit
of poetry in sadness

and very little wrong
that I can see,
so I stake out boundaries,

then am still to let
the answers come.
When I walk in the rain

electricity gets through.
Festivals and hammers
are to blame for making

noise, but I'm silent
in my scarcity, know
things that don't belong

here, or in the grass—weapons
in the leaves. I'm not
of the forest, not simple

like an ornament.
I think in the feminine:
curve and skin, the shoulder

that turns into your hands
and all the days.
The birds remind me

every time—you must consider
the branch falling,
but consider it from the tree.

Equilibrium

I take balance seriously, but then
there are the issues of the moment:

I attend to the food bowl and the news,
the small tasks that persuade me,

though I'd rather recline
on an easy chair, watch the rain

wave the window, memorize the patterns
of the chintz, even if those flowers

are flat and nothing like 3-D, still life
in fabric that shut out the day's dark.

No more kettle, no more scalpel blade:
the instruments forget to reconnoiter.

So there may be chaos or an orderly
procession of business and wine.

Say you're only staying until intermission,
want to miss the last half

of everything—operas, books, the sorry
grade-school play—so you'd have twice

the time, could do more and never
be disappointed by endings.

Maybe the branches' tapestry
against the sky is stitching apart,

and maybe the rain's long French kiss
excites them, but I can't know, can't guess

exactly how anything exists outside
my own body, busy all the time

trying to recover from gin and tonics,
the injuries of love and wondering.

All the sorcerers agree:
the hardest trick is making sure

the magic wants to be performed.
And endings can be a kind of magic

so I'm telling the trees to remember,
promising that their last half of standing

must be witnessed by someone else.
Watch over me, my level, my slippery eel,

demon who comes to me all night holding
out a miracle—and shouldn't I tell you?—

balance won't help the if, if, if
of my beating heart, the steady questing thuds.

Reaching Danger

Safe is not a concept I relate to
anymore, since all the rungs of my ladder
are broken. The chimney hasn't been cleaned

in years. Every sniffle on the subway
could be Ebola, could be infection
whispering into an ear, but I am hoping

to go down the road of danger, all
the way to the end, past peril waving
from the shoulder, past jeopardy and hazard.

I see the vulnerable ride bicycles, I see tanning beds
and cars. Safety suffers here—it's fed
the rind of watermelon and escorted

into the dark. At this point, I might say
anything: that love may need oxygen,
but I'm not breathing. That certain passages

in Marx remind me of figs, seeds like that,
thickly taking over. This wouldn't be a lie:
I am on to how everything connects

to all other things, in some way, at some time,
and how smoke and mirrors possess power.
Trust, but verify. All the times you came up

empty, told the fox and the chipmunk lonely,
lonely, willed the parachute to open in the glands,
watched orgies and petit theft, come back now.

I'm here, and at the edge. Simplify
and leaving are words I can say. I can also say
secret and heaven and sinking. Demands

that float you, guide you into seeing
the mosaic in sand, the stump rendering itself.
Cup is to blood is to definition. I say tea

and vein and word. And word inside
itself. If I say prison and domicile,
I weather. I steep. I stray and stray.

Ghost Ships

Or the decline of the Roman Empire
was a burlesque: the show you can't avoid,
the manner of speaking that wings its way

into the core of the apple, a reminder
of the balloon and the thistle, the down
comforter that drapes over the recklessness

I call my life: I am covered in the hues
of meaning, in the varied nuances
of septic tanks and swingsets.

And it's a different way of speaking: you can't
understand loss without losing something,
can't read a book in the dark. Open me

to any page and the words will look familiar:
I am no cipher, no puzzle, no babbling brook.
The ends of the chain provoke you

to connection, and that can't be
an accident, either, unless accident means
the will to explain is lost—why not

the beautiful words of desire to accompany
forgiveness and grief, or the everyday sounds
of dishes in the sink, the turnstile, the jet

engine? I could hear you over the din,
in the deepest cave, in the recesses of childhood,
those paths that foretold us.

Here's truth in the sunset and a cold beer,
but it isn't the only truth: you want me
to be a riddle, but I am only a sum.

I am watching myself from the margins,
waiting for some cataclysm or sign—
you can't reach me from where you are,

and I can't answer the questions I pose,
but you can: how long will a cord of wood
last if no one tends the fire?

I'm thinking that the heart's orchestra
practices in middle age. And am I middle-aged
now, when I finally seem to walk inside

myself, to know the dangers of being
and having, of not doing and regrets?
The only harness in this world

is this sustained hearkening of the heart—
a witness and a key—where I am standing.
Which reminds me: stay. I know

the rule is to deny. I know the practice
is to pretend nothing happened, to force
out of the chambers a note that isn't heard

elsewhere. Yet the moss. Yet the swift crosses
the sky, a perfect geometry, an augmentation
of order. Don't reprimand me for not knowing,

for swallowing the truth whole—
You can't be here. What if we're ghost ships?
What if we sail right past each other?

Sunday Lyric

If only the night would resolve.
If only there were a diagnosis
for this resolution: to stand
apart and charge the destiny of words.
I know the touch of dogma and the
opinion of the moon when the map
sheds a country. A door will close
tomorrow, and I already love
its memory—I'm tending
a garden of honey, a field of corn,
and will they imitate me
in their loneliness? You must know
you'll carry one cell of my heart,
a reminder that the word
was yes, and even in the dignified
motions of saying hello or farewell,
there's always again. Soon
there's only sky to bind us
to the repeating days, to other nights
that really matter, to the wheat field
of crows giving up and taking
their hard wings into the wind.

Prayer

May these blossoms ignite in your trees.
May tresses of wind fall
across your back. May irrational sculpture
greet you each morning.

Here's a relic in this aftermath:
the meaning of roses and falling
into the truth when the wind walks
through the scene: may it be.

May you discover it's time to speak
openly. May you never feel betrayed,
never tread this near pathology.
Listen, all my conclusions came

from faulty syllogisms, so may I see
what's under the score, and may I not
perform this music with my eyes closed.
My skull chants with it, even

among the songs of birds. May there be
a way to be without, and a way to erase
what never happened. May you know
the fragility of make-believe.

After the Cocktail Hours

You left me to clean up the assorted messes
we'd both made, but I don't resent it,
even while I remember how dustpans
of Cheerios and brooms of webs
appeared in my hands like debt.
I don't blame you. It's nearly evening

and the sky is turning down its light.
I know you are waiting at the switch,
your hands full of shot-glass and bottle
for the all-clear. You've made it
past five o'clock. Another cruelty:
your eyes, with their stirrings

and wanderings. I wanted to lie down
in them and pull your lids over me.
I wanted, forgive me, to drown in them.
What's left is one gardenia and a
watering can filled with silk.
I don't resent holding your hair

behind you. I don't resent the moon
when it makes its slow passes.
There's something about light
and whiskey and pine trees
that clarify the night, as if we'd left it
boiling on the stove. I didn't know

you were a desert. I didn't know I was
a nomad. Some things can't be
helped: they'll pull an arm
behind your back and whisper,
your money or your life, and by God,
sometimes the money's worth more.

Words a Hospitality

An oasis can spring up in the actual
dark—consider the pineapple,

its hospitality and form, that faceless
baby crying welcome. It isn't much

that you are offered peace, but it's enough
to keep and hold, even while parasites

practice the natural process of living.
Today the wind infects my consciousness

with sound: I stay away from radios,
block my ears with cotton. Surely

there's a shore across the ocean that summons
you, and a whistle blowing somewhere

down the street. Make the sun turn
its head to evening, make Spanish moss

and maples rest, so everyone
can wander to the seaside, dig clams

or skip rocks. Be.
Be is the state I'm reaching for,

though in that I suppose I'm failing—
I am not and am not, though often

there is consequence. In the garden
snails smooth across the stones

and you must be slow to follow them.
And provide hot cups of tea

for company, for visitors who depart
before they arrive. I wonder about the mice

I hear and the courtesies that require the voice
of hunger nailing at the door. Too rebuked

the heart. So I'm stopping in the silk tent
I see in dreams—your face on every citizen,

your hands an invitation I accept.
But isn't this the way that memory mourns?

One thing replaces another and so on
and so on until, like the layers of our skin

that shed themselves, your whole
updates again. In the aperture of grief,

I take a picture of the past, when it didn't help
to be reminded that textures and pomegranates

can mean the same thing, if the light is right,
the brain floating lovely in its preservation. Forget

the first-grade teacher's name, the slogans carved
in desks. Torsion is defined in part by force:

if one day the brave glance betrays you,
it's process you can blame: the look

foretold and every pattern blanking out,
the faithless end of bruise and bite and hold.

How Time Passes in the Middle Age

I shouldn't know these things yet:
the deaths and mortgages, the decaying flesh.
But I do, so all my friends are older—

it's better that way. I can relate to them.
Still the empires of consciousness
embrace me. Still the winds of youth
bluster past. I am unmoved. I am immovable.

If I told you the story of paint,
how it evolved from the art
of the patterns of wounds, could you believe?

Oh, my God, I'm doing it again: watching

the day eat its tail, seeing myself abscond
into the years; no happy ending, knowing,
as I do, the life cycle of the cattail, the story
of the bees. This muddy road
has a thousand places to step, a hundred
ways to ruin a pump. And dirt
is what it's all about, isn't it?

The ash, the gossip. An odalisque reclining
on a brass bed. Most of the time
I'm not even sure of my own name,

which will be changing, which will
have changed. There are other narrators.

There are other dimensions. The force
of anger is good. The force of happiness

is missing, flown and gone, swept
into the river that is a river.

And can't everything stand
for everything else? Bird for love,
tree for security, truth for a long ride
in a hot car—the days become older, too.
It's just like time to age you,

to build another you on the outside
of your young body, which you remember
from time to time as being still here,
still able to dance all night, drink
big men under the table, and bluff,
a lot, at the weekly poker game.

I shouldn't know this either: it's not true
anymore that time passes
slowly—it's sped up, on fast forward,
the remote in someone else's hand,
finger on the button and a grim apology.

Coming Apart, Together

We're all coming home now
for the funerals, saying goodbye
to the last gnarls, watching earth
spaded back into earth
in February's short light
or the longer ease of June.

I can't hear anything but the noise
of fifty harps, all those nails pounded.
Sounds are ribbons tying
me to what's left now: some sort
of water or doorway, shades
of pink in sugared night.

It doesn't matter that teeth
and bones and hair scatter
in the gravel we walk over
to the most recent grave,
temporary marker
and drying flowers as good

as neon signs: your
parents and mine will rest here,
forever, or at least longer
than we'll know about,
and that will have to do.
We'll go home to the dark

and light it, then float
in some suspended state
like sleep, or what sleep would be
if it grabbed you by the hair,
pulled you down where meaning
travels an unmarked road.

The mower and the backhoe argue
in the background like flies,
and maybe I've used my quota
of grief, or of words. The circuit
breakers sit quietly,
in the dark, and I know fire

is breaking out somewhere tonight.
I watch more riots
of chrysanthemum and rose,
sprays bound together with gold-
script: *Father, Mother, Sister,
Brother, Your Name Here.*

Spring Burials

We were waiting for a thaw.
The plots were tiny, the bones small.
We spaded the earth over itself for
hamsters, the parakeets, a cat.

There is nothing left here
of the people who called this home,
nor of the careful plan of the garden.
Another family mows the yard.

Pine needles thatch the ground.
A tiny egg falls from a nest, and against
the years, I find it, carry it around
the yard. I don't yet know

it will never be a bird. Other lessons
happen: training wheels, traffic,
secrets that shouldn't be.
The neighbors' kids grow up

and move away, cars are traded in.
Then, the light from the stars
of those nights arrives here.
Across the ravine between me

and those years are the voices
that called me in to dinner, that shrieked
in the spring air. I hear them
make the sound of my name.

Maybe I shouldn't tell you this.
Maybe by letting you know me,
I diminish myself somehow and become
smaller than my pets' bones buried

in the yard. But if disclosure is damage,
I don't know what else there is.
How else can we connect
in what we earn of these brief

and terrible days? So I want you
to have this: the yellow of the forsythia
on the hill in my backyard, year
after year, and my mother scrambling

down the hill, the gardening shears
in her right hand. She grasps branches.
Cuts. Comes back up the hill
by the path next to where the animals rest.

She arranges the flowers in a crystal vase,
sets it on the piano in the living room,
then puts the shears into the kitchen's
narrow junk drawer. She hums

to me across this afternoon's silence.

Apples and Oranges

How you meant to compare the orange
and the apple was a failure, but you don't know

that yet, since you're still concentrating
on size and shape and color, forgetting

that essence is the fulcrum, the component
of each that defines what and how, but chiefly

why, since the comparison is ridiculous—we all know
that. Once, in a candy store, on display

the very same objects—apples and oranges—
but then the sugar and hunger and general

in-commonness made you pause. You're tender
when you think of fruit, know

the proper names for parts,
the structures that separate and sweeten

until the drop from the tree.
If it isn't fruit, it's another similarity—

differences disturb you. Unlikeness
speaks to you in tongues. I want to point

out how everything's eaten, everything eats;
I've heard this and believe it's true,

that no matter how similar or different
the subject, the outcome is the same.

You eat the apple. The orange eats you,
in some elemental way, anyway,

since I'm not a literalist, but can't relate
to surreal distinctions

between cups of fur and the buttons of air
you fasten on your coat of aluminum

and bacon grease. So there's a tree,
an orange tree, heavy with the confetti

of citrus that will fall and be gathered,
taken to the market, sold, then eaten

by celebrants—it isn't rocket science,
this simple fruit that ripens

and becomes an ornament
before it finds its way

to your Waldorf salad or a child's hand.
But it's not nothing, either, and not

something to compare to anything else—
not concepts of production, or profits

or loss—but real fruit in a real mouth,
its real juice running orangely down the chin.

Revisiting Gauguin

I hold the lowest leaves
of the banana tree in my left hand.
I tousle your hair with the other.
The sounds of the jungle

encroach, ride up our spines
in the night's early air. If you're out
of green, the blue will do—blue fronds,
blue sand, and a halo of blue flame

around my waist. Too many names
I can't remember—Pasteur, or was it Pavlov,
who made me salivate just by thinking
of me? There is nothing

quite as lovely as a trapped wasp,
the windowpane a warm beckoning.
But it isn't to be. The clincher:
old growth and mustard seeds, things

we hand down, but what if your
descendents die before you?
They stagger up the cellar stairs
in mutton chops and ringlets,

linen and wool. Wouldn't know
a keyboard from a microwave
from a radio from a Buick.
Most nights, their tapping dies away

after a while. Most nights
your offspring and their offspring
content themselves playing whist
or considering how shameful

the movements of the waltz.
There are tasks to occupy them:
emptying the commode, banking
the night's fire. Already

their rapping on the cellar door
is muffled, halfhearted. Their plans
for the future almost never include you.
Do not forget: spring has heated the wasps

to a manageable warmth, so they march
on their glass fields, devising.
Mondays, the milk truck chirps backwards
into the driveway. Mornings, it may still

decide to rain. It's possible this is all
a movie set. What if the only way
to ensure your traits is to take by force
things not meant for you? Will you dive

into those waters? Will you peel
the beautiful rind from the fruit?
And afterward, will you sometimes wish
you could paint yourself back into the garden?

Never-Never

Never simple: into the night, all the day's light
turning into less, into a moon that studies
its stars and wants forgiveness.

And never the rat, never the sewer or drain.
Never the plasma dripping into the bag.
Never the hush of thieves

in a dark foyer—never this one, never the other,
never molting or shedding skin, even if it's time.
Never Jello, never rice. Never iron, never grief.

Never sadness, never dues, never me. Never
the trumpet vine or the daffodil, never tendrils
of want and heat. Never mooring at a quay.

Never sowing the ashes into dirt, into bone-bits
and wrought iron, never seeking what isn't there.
Never minding rain or the other caprices of weather.

Never loosening the lid of a stuck jar, never sailing.
Never naming trees. Never ordering the meals
or deaths of many men. Never stunning a fly

before you kill it—never touching someone's skin
you want as a part of your own. Never worshiping
another house of cards. Never eating cereal or crow.

Never matching the numbers. Never spending
time on wasting it. Never pardoning
yourself and never letting go. Never knowing orange,

never anger over fury: I am loose in myself
and stalk. I can't catch what I can't find.
In the relentless clouds, a dream: buttons never falling

from the sky, never landing on highways and the open
faces of animals who depend on me. I watch the walls
fall, even want them to: I know the risks inside

the snow globe—the shaking that takes place.
I never, never meant to solidify the space between
sorrow and the future. But it's here: meet

and tidy in its formlessness. It's everything. It's nothing.
It's the future or it's not. It will find me if I let it.
May I never, never know what will never happen.

Working Through the Codes

God, there are so many ways to die
or fail, and I'm reading
through the Workers' Comp Diagnosis Codes—
8.1 *Arizona Enteritis*, 427.32 *Atrial Flutter*—

wondering how, when all these pitfalls
exist, I've managed to avoid so many.
I've never been afflicted
with 364.51 *Progressive Iris Atrophy*

or 115 *Histoplasmosis,* though I have cats
and eyes. Nor have I experienced 300.13
Psychogenic Fugue (that I know of, but
would I know?), nor, thank you,

13.3 *Tubercular Abscess of the Brain*,
and thanks once more, just to make sure.
I'd be distressed by 717 *Internal Derangement
of the Knee*, 736.21 *Boutonniere Deformity*,

748.2 *Laryngeal Web*, and I suspect by
784.6 *Other Symbolic Dysfunction.*
I think I may have had 750 *Tongue Tie* once,
but really my damage has been limited to diseases

harmless or operable—226 *Benign Neoplasm,
Thyroid*, 190.6 *Malignant Neoplasm,
Choroid*, 366.46 *Cataract with Radiation*—
conditions the knife can cut out

or lumps that can stay in me. I don't mind
that there are abnormal groups of cells
congregating in my neck as long as
I can avoid 312.34 *Intermittent Explosive*

Disorder, 203 *Multiple Myeloma*, 718.3
Recurrent Dislocation, and definitely 780 *Coma
and Stupor*, though sometimes
I go around like that for fun.

My Compass Will Not Orient

Whatever I thought about when things started
to get complicated doesn't matter now—
so this scene is all about politeness,
about making sure the hostess knows
the punch was good, the crackers fresh,
that even though all the conversations

were boring, they were at least civil,
too, and stopped us from acting
like ourselves—as we are at home in the robe,
feet up on the coffee table's rim, crumbs
falling from the corners of our mouths
like ducks shot by someone with true aim.

In college, when my advisor asked
Do you like to be outside? Do you like
to read maps?, I signed up for Orienteering.
Every week we'd drive miles in a van,
pile out at the state park and set off
into the woods. My compass always stuck,

North was always North, no matter
which way my body turned,
so the tiny flags hidden earlier among
the trees always went undiscovered.
And did I mention this was timed?
Late in the semester, looking down

once more at the useless instrument,
the vast nothing before me, running,
running, across logs and rotting twigs,
I tumbled into the carcass of a deer,
half-decayed, its ribcage a mound
of fur and leaves, my foot in its belly

like some bizarre still-life Kung Fu,
I finally learned the lesson of the course:
having a direction is always an accident,
a way to decide, when you step
in something, the best way to extricate
yourself to cause the least damage.

For the Cormorants Whose Necks Are Loosely Tied with String So They May Not Swallow Their Catch

It must disappoint them to find
the fish will not go smoothly
down the throat, will not go down

at all, even after the glare on the water
softens to reveal what looks like dinner
moving beneath the surface, even

after the bill is full, the weight expanding
the pouch like the loose upper arms
of a grandmother on a farm near Wichita.

She reaches under the hens each day, walks
back to the house with a basket
of white sunrise. The planet revolves.

Cooks tie kerchiefs under their chins.
A million skillets crackle under bacon
and eggs. A continent away, the refuge

attracts a third-grade class. They wing
it across the preserve's dry flats and yell
when they spot a new species, telltale

markings the code to distinguishing
between—what? Between two birds
whose genetic material is so close

that their body shapes, their wingspans,
their very swallowness or killdeerness
depends a little on perception and longing.

A yellow-headed blackbird lifts
above the reeds, startles a boy into turning
his head. And it's enough—it's that

astonishing—that small change in trajectory
that will remind him all his life
how insignificant his decisions—to the planet,

to the mountains and estuaries and oceans,
to migratory and mating rituals—he's not
responsible for changing anything but himself,

not ever, even though in this, his one life,
he's never approached the bird and snugged
the string. He hasn't untied it, either, and

when the birds travel low, ripples spread over
the surface of the water in some sympathetic
pantomime of the vibrations the strings make

around the cormorants' necks each time they
find, once again, that their lives have turned into
someone else's dinner, someone else's flight.